Southampt Quiz Book

101 Fun and Interesting Questions
To Test Your Knowledge
of Southampton Football Club

Published by Glowworm Press
7 Nuffield Way
Abingdon OX14 1RL

By Chris Carpenter

Southampton Football Club

This Southampton Football Club quiz book contains one hundred and one informative and entertaining trivia questions, all with multiple choice answers. Some questions are easy, and some are quite challenging, and this book is guaranteed to test your knowledge and memory of the club's history.

You will be asked a variety of questions on a wide range of topics associated with Southampton FC for you to test yourself. You will be quizzed on players, legends, managers, opponents, transfer deals, trophies, records, honours, fixtures, terrace songs and much more, guaranteeing you both an educational and fun read. Informative, enjoyable and fun, this quiz book will test your knowledge of **Southampton Football Club** and prove you know the club's history.

2020/21 Season Edition

FOREWORD

When I was asked to write a foreword to this book I was flattered.

I have known the author Chris Carpenter for a number of years and his knowledge of facts and figures is phenomenal.

His love for football and his skill in writing quiz books make him the ideal man to pay homage to my great love Southampton Football Club.

This book came about as a result of a challenge on a golf course.

I do hope you enjoy the book.

Doug Terrie

Let's start with some relatively easy questions.

1. When were Southampton founded?
   A. 1902
   B. 1885
   C. 1890

2. What is Southampton's nickname?
   A. The Magpies
   B. The Saints
   C. The Spurs

3. Where does Southampton play their home games?
   A. The Dell
   B. Selhurst Park
   C. St Mary's Stadium

4. What is the stadium's capacity?
   A. 32,384
   B. 32,438
   C. 32,843

5. Who or what is the club mascot?
   A. Sammy Saint
   B. Scary Saint
   C. Stokie Saint

6. Who has made the most appearances for the club in total?
   A. Rickie Lambert
   B. Matthew Le Tissier
   C. Terry Paine

7. Who is the club's record goal scorer?
   A. Mick Channon
   B. Ron Davies
   C. Bill Rawlings

8. Who is the fastest ever goal scorer for the club?
   A. Ron Davies
   B. Derek Reeves
   C. Douglas McGibbon

9. What song do the players run out to?
   A. When the Saints Go Marching In
   B. Simply The Best
   C. Go South

10. Which of these is a well known pub near the ground?
   A. Iso Tavern
   B. Kings Bar
   C. Waterfront Bar

OK, here are the answers to the first ten questions. If you get eight or more right, you are doing well, but be warned, the questions will get harder.

A1. Southampton were founded on the 21st November 1885.

A2. The official nickname of Southampton is 'The Saints'.

A3. After many years at The Dell, Southampton now play their home games at St Mary's Stadium.

A4. The current stadium capacity is 32,384.

A5. The club mascot is a dog called Sammy Saint. Give yourself a bonus point if you know he has a twin called Super Saint!

A6. Terry Paine has made the most appearances for the club. He played in 809 first-team matches in total from1956 to 1974.

A7. Mick Channon is the club's record scorer with 227 goals. Legend.

A8. Douglas McGibbon is the fastest ever goal scorer for the club. He scored a goal just 4.6 seconds after kick off in a match against Chelsea on 29th December 1945.

A9. The players run out to 'When the Saints Go Marching In'.

A10. The Waterfront Bar is a well known pub near the ground. Be prepared to queue for a pint though.

OK, back to the questions.

11. What is the highest number of goals that Southampton has scored in a league season?
    A. 120
    B. 118
    C. 112

12. What is the fewest number of goals that Southampton has conceded in a league season?
    A. 31
    B. 25
    C. 21

13. Who has scored the most penalties for the club?
    A. James Beattie
    B. Matt Le Tissier
    C. Ricky Lambert

14. Who has made the most Premier League appearances for the club?
    A. Jason Dodd
    B. Matt Oakley
    C. Matt Le Tissier

15. Where are the away supporters seated in the ground?
    A. Chapel Stand
    B. Itchen Stand
    C. North Stand

16. What is the club's record attendance at the new ground?
    A. 31,727
    B. 32,363
    C. 33,549

17. Where is Southampton's training ground?
    A. Finch Farm
    B. Motspur Park
    C. Staplewood

18. What is the name of the road the ground is on?
    A. Britannia Road
    B. Coventry Road
    C. Kings Road

19. Which is the main stand of the ground?
    A. Chapel Stand
    B. Itchen Stand
    C. Kingsland Stand

20. What is the size of the pitch?
    A. 112 x 74 yards
    B. 114 x 72 yards
    C. 116 x 70 yards

Here are the answers to the last set of questions.

A11. The highest number of goals that Southampton has scored in a league season is 112. They achieved this feat in the 1957/58 season.

A12. The fewest number of goals that Southampton has conceded in a league season is 21. They achieved this in the 1921/22 season.

A13. Matt Le Tissier scored 47 penalties for the club. 47 in 48 attempts!

A14. With 329 Premier League appearances, Jason Dodd holds the record for the Premier League appearances for the club.

A15. Away supporters are seated in the North Stand.

A16. The club's record attendance at the new stadium is 32,363 in a crucial game against Coventry City on 28th April 2012, when the club won 4-0 and sealed promotion to the Premier League.

A17. Southampton's training ground is located in Staplewood.

A18. The ground is located on Britannia Road.

A19. The Itchen Stand (named after the River Itchen) is the main stand of the ground. The stand also houses the club's offices, changing rooms, press facilities, 42 executive boxes, and a number of corporate hospitality suites.

A20. The size of the pitch is 112 yards long by 74 yards wide. By way of comparison, Wembley's pitch is 115 yards long by 75 yards wide.

Now we move onto some questions about some of the club's records.

21. What is the club's record win in any competition?
    A. 10-0
    B. 12-0
    C. 14-0

22. Who did they beat?
    A. Newbury Town
    B. Plymouth Argyle
    C. Watford

23. In which year?
    A. 1890
    B. 1892
    C. 1894

24. What is the club's record win in the Premier League?
    A. 6-0
    B. 6-2
    C. 6-3

25. Who did they beat?
    A. Manchester United
    B. Middlesbrough
    C. Swindon Town

26. In which season?
    A. 1992/93
    B. 1994/95

C. 1996/97

27. What is the club's record defeat in the
    First Division?
        A. 0-8
        B. 0-9
        C. 0-10

28. Who against?
        A. Arsenal
        B. Chelsea
        C. Everton

29. In which season?
        A. 1957/58
        B. 1964/65
        C. 1971/72

30. Who has scored the most hat tricks for
    Southampton?
        A. James Beattie
        B. Matt Le Tissier
        C. Alan Shearer

Here are the answers to the last set of questions.

A21. The club's record win in any competition is 14-0.

A22. The club beat Newbury Town 14-0 in an FA Cup qualifying round. It was an official match, so that is why it is in the record books.

A23. The match took place on 13th October 1894, so it is the 1894/85 season.

A24. The club's record win in the Premier League is 6-3.

A25. Southampton defeated Manchester United 6-3 in its record victory. United manager Ferguson couldn't blame the defeat on grey shirts for this one, as United played in blue and white stripes on the day.

A26. The match took place on 26th October 1996; so, it was in the 1996/97 season.

A27. The club's record defeat in the First Division is 0-8.

A28. The club's record defeat came against Everton.

A29. The match was played on 20th November 1971 so it was during the 1971/72 season.

A30. Matt Le Tissier scored the most hat tricks for Southampton. He scored four hat tricks for the club in total.

Now we move onto the next set of questions.

31. How many times have Southampton won the FA Cup?
    A. 0
    B. 1
    C. 2

32. How many times have Southampton won the Southern League?
    A. 4
    B. 5
    C. 6

33. What is the furthest that the club has progressed in the League Cup?
    A. Quarter-final
    B. Semi-final
    C. Final

34. Who was the captain when the club reached that far in The League Cup?
    A. Alan Ball
    B. Chris Nicholl
    C. David Peach

35. When did the club win the FA Cup?
    A. 1972
    B. 1974
    C. 1976

36. Who did they beat in the Final?
    A. Arsenal

B. Manchester United
C. Wolverhampton Wanderers

37. What was the score?
    A. 2-0
    B. 2-1
    C. 1-0

38. Who was the captain who lifted the FA Cup?
    A. Martin Chivers
    B. Bill Rawlings
    C. Peter Rodrigues

39. Who was the manager that day?
    A. Ted Bates
    B. Lawrie McMenemy
    C. Chris Nicholl

40. How many Englishmen started that day?
    A. 2
    B. 5
    C. 8

Here are the answers to the last block of questions.

A31. The club has won the FA Cup once in its history.

A32. Southampton has won the Southern League a total of six times.

A33. The club progressed to the final of the League Cup in 1979. Unfortunately, they lost to Nottingham Forest 2-3.

A34. Alan Ball was captain of the Southampton side when they reached the League Cup Final in 1979.

A35. The club won its one and only FA Cup in 1976.

A36. They beat Manchester United in the final at Wembley Stadium on 1st May 1976. Southampton finished sixth in the Second Division that season and were every much the underdogs against Manchester United who had finished third in the First Division.

A37. The score was 1-0, with Bobby Stokes the scorer in the 83rd minute.

A38. Welshman Peter Rodrigues was the Saints captain who lifted the FA Cup on that glorious spring day.

A39. Lawrie McMenemy was the Southampton manager that season.

A40. Of the eleven players who started, 8 were English, 2 Scottish and 1 Welsh. The substitute was Scottish. How times have changed!

I hope you're having fun, and getting most of the answers right.

41. What is the record transfer fee paid?
    A. £18 million
    B. £19 million
    C. £20 million

42. Who was the record transfer fee paid for?
    A. Guido Carillo
    B. Danny Ings
    C. Mario Lemina

43. What is the record transfer fee received?
    A. £71 million
    B. £73 million
    C. £75 million

44. Who was the record transfer fee received for?
    A. Adam Lallana
    B. Sadio Mane
    C. Virgil van Dijk

45. Who was the first Southampton player to play for England?
    A. Ron Davies
    B. Terry Paine
    C. Bill Rawlings

46. Who has won the most international caps whilst a Southampton player?
   A. Chris Nicholl
   B. Marian Pahars
   C. Peter Shilton

47. Who has scored the most international goals whilst a Southampton player?
   A. Mick Channon
   B. Ron Davies
   C. Anders Svensson

48. Who is the youngest player ever to represent the club?
   A. Callum Chambers
   B. Luke Shaw
   C. Theo Walcott

49. Who is the oldest player ever to represent the club?
   A. Kelvin Davis
   B. Bruce Grobbelaar
   C. Kevin Moore

50. Who is the club captain for the 2020/21 season?
   A. Ryan Bertrand
   B. Jannik Vestergaard
   C. James Ward-Prowse

Here are the answers to the last set of questions.

A41. The record transfer fee paid is £20 million to Liverpool for a striker.

A42. Danny Ings was bought from Liverpool for an initial £18 million in July 2019 and after successfully meeting various targets in the contract, the figure rose to £20 million, so he is now Southampton's record transfer. The fee of £20 million eclipses the previous record of £19 million paid for Argentinian forward Guido Carillo in January 2018 who played just ten games (without scoring) for the club before being loaned out at the end of the season.

A43. The record transfer fee received by the club is £75 million.

A44. The fee was received for Virgil van Dijk from Liverpool in January 2018.

A45. Terry Paine was the first Southampton player to play for England. He played for England in 1966.

A46. Peter Shilton won the most international caps whilst a Southampton player. He won 50 caps for England while playing for the club between 1982 and 1987.

A47. Mick Channon scored the most international goals whilst a Southampton player. He scored 21 goals from 45 appearances for England.

A48. Theo Walcott is the youngest player ever to represent the club. He played at the age of 16 years 143 days against Wolverhampton Wanderers on 6th August 2005.

A49. Bruce Grobbelaar is the oldest player ever to represent the club. He appeared against Aston Villa on 8th April 1996 at the age of 38 years and 184 days.

A50. For the 2020/21 season James Ward-Prowse has the role of club captain.

I hope you're learning some new facts about the Saints.

51. What is the highest number of draws that the club has had in a season?
    A. 15
    B. 17
    C. 19

52. Who is the club's longest serving manager of all time?
    A. Ted Bates
    B. Alfred McMinn
    C. George Swift

53. Who is the club's longest serving post war manager?
    A. Ernest Arnfield
    B. Ted Bates
    C. Alan Pardew

54. What is the name of the Southampton match day programme?
    A. Saints
    B. Southampton FC Matchday programme
    C. Southampton Days

55. What is the club's official twitter account?
    A. @Saints
    B. @Southampton
    C. @SouthamptonFC

56. Which of these is a Southampton fanzine?
    A. Gate18
    B. Marching Saints
    C. The Ugly Inside

57. What is on the club crest?
    A. White Flag
    B. White Peacock
    C. White Rose

58. What is the club's motto?
    A. Pluribus Maximus
    B. Superbia in proelia
    C. There is no motto

59. Who is considered as Southampton's main rivals?
    A. Bournemouth
    B. Brighton
    C. Portsmouth

60. What could be regarded as the club's most well known song?
    A. Shine On You Crazy Saints
    B. We Are Up For It
    C. When The Saints Go Marching In

Here are the answers to the last set of questions.

A51. Southampton had a staggering 19 draws in the 2005/06 season.

A52. Ted Bates is the club's longest serving manager of all time. He managed the club for 18 years and 2 months from September 1955 to November 1973.

A53. Ted Bates is also the club's longest serving post war manager.

A54. The catchy name of the programme is Saints.

A55. @SouthamptonFC is the club's official twitter account. It tweets multiple times daily and it has over a million followers.

A56. The Ugly Inside is probably the best known Southampton fanzine.

A57. A white rose is present on the club's crest. The rose is the symbol of the city which is also present on the city's coat of arms.

A58. There is no official club motto.

A59. Portsmouth is considered as Southampton's main rivals. The matches between the two sides are known as the South Coast Derby.

A60. "When The Saints Go Marching In" can be regarded as the club's most well known song.

Let's give you some easier questions.

61. What is the traditional colour of the home shirt?
    A. Red and black stripes
    B. Red and white stripes
    C. Red and yellow stripes

62. What is the traditional colour of the away shirt?
    A. Blue
    B. Green
    C. Pink

63. Who is the current club sponsor?
    A. LD Sports
    B. Sportsbet.io
    C. Virgin Media

64. Who was the first club sponsor?
    A. Dimplex
    B. Draper Tools
    C. Rank Xerox

65. Which of these airlines have sponsored the club?
    A. British Airways
    B. FlyBe
    C. Virgin Atlantic

66. Who is currently the club chairman?
    A. Nicola Cortese
    B. Ralph Krueger

C. Rupert Lowe

67. How many goals did Ron Davies score
    for Southampton?
    A. 118
    B. 126
    C. 134

68. Who started the 2019/20 season as
    manager?
    A. Mark Hughes
    B. Mauricio Pellegrino
    C. Ralph Hasenhuttl

69. Who started the 2019/20 season as
    goalkeeping coach?
    A. Craig Fleming
    B. Andrew Sparkes
    C. David Watson

70. Who was the club's first match in the
    Premier League against?
    A. Leeds United
    B. Manchester City
    C. Tottenham Hotspur

Here are the answers to the last set of questions.

A61. The traditional colour of the home shirt is red and white stripes

A62. The traditional colour of the away shirt is a tricky one, as the club have worn all sorts of colours over the years including black, beige, blue, green, grey, white and yellow. Give yourself a point if you didn't say pink.

A63. Sportsbet.io is the current club sponsor. They signed a one year deal in August 2020.

A64. The first company to sponsor the club was photocopier manufacturer Rank Xerox who sponsored the club for three years from 1980.

A65. FlyBe sponsored Southampton from 2006 to 2010. Give yourself a bonus point if you knew that Air Florida once sponsored the club (during the 1983/84 season).

A66. Chinese businessman Gao Jishen is the current club chairman.

A67. Ron Davies scored 134 goals for Southampton.

A68. Ralph Hasenhuttl started the 2020/21 season as manager, having been appointed to the role in December 2018.

A69. Andrew Sparkes started the 2020/21 season as goalkeeping coach.

A70. The club were founder members of the Premier League and their first game was a goalless draw at home to Tottenham Hotspur on the 15th August 1992.

Here is the next batch of ten carefully chosen questions.

71. Who is Southampton's highest ever goal scorer in the Premier League?
    A. James Beattie
    B. Rickie Lambert
    C. Matt Le Tissier

72. Who holds the record for most goals scored in a season for the club?
    A. James Beattie
    B. Egil Ostenstad
    C. Derek Reeves

73. Who holds the record of scoring in all the 34 penalty kicks he took for the club?
    A. Adam Lallana
    B. Rickie Lambert
    C. Matt Le Tissier

74. What is the west stand of the ground also known as?
    A. Chapel
    B. Itchen
    C. Kingsland

75. Who raised £1 million for charity by doing five ironman events?
    A. Francis Benali
    B. Ken Monkou
    C. Matt Oakley

76. What is the current state of the Dell?
    A. Allotments
    B. Housing
    C. Shopping centre

77. How many Premier League goals did
    Marian Pahars score for the club?
    A. 22
    B. 32
    C. 42

78. What was Matt Le Tissier's nickname?
    A. Le Frog
    B. Le God
    C. Le Winger

79. Who is the club's youngest ever Premier
    League player?
    A. Calum Chambers
    B. Matt Oakley
    C. Luke Shaw

80. Who was the leading goalscorer for the
    2019/20 season?
    A. Stuart Armstrong
    B. Danny Ings
    C. Nathan Redmond

Here are the answers to the last set of questions.

A71. Matt Le Tissier is Southampton's highest ever goal scorer in the Premier League with 101 goals. James Beattie is a long way behind with 68.

A72. Derek Reeves is the club's record goal scorer in one season, netting 43 times in the 1959/60 season.

A73. Rickie Lambert holds the record of scoring in all the 34 penalty kicks he took for the club.

A74. The west stand of the ground is known as the Kingsland Stand.

A75. In April 2019, Francis Benali completed five ironman marathons in five days, and raised over £1 million for Cancer Research UK for his efforts.

A76. The Dell was demolished in 2001, and there is now a housing estate where the ground used to be.

A77. Marian Pahars scored 42 Premier League goals for the club.

A78. The fans nicknamed Le Tissier 'Le God'.

A79. Luke Shaw is the youngest ever Premier League player for the club. He made his debut aged just 17 years and 117 days against West Bromwich Albion on 5th November 2012.

A80. Danny Ings was the leading goalscorer for the 2019/20 season, scoring 25 times in all competitions, including 22 in the league.

Here are the next set of questions, let's hope you get most of them right.

81. Who has scored the most goals in one match for Southampton?
    A. Albert Brown
    B. Terry Paine
    C. Derek Reeves

82. How many times did Matt Le Tissier win the Player of the Year award?
    A. 1
    B. 2
    C. 3

83. Who scored the fastest goal on Premier League history in April 2019?
    A. Stuart Armstrong
    B. Charlie Austin
    C. Shane Long

84. Who is the official kit supplier to the club?
    A. Adidas
    B. Umbro
    C. Under Armour

85. Which famous musician has played twice at the stadium?
    A. Bon Jovi
    B. Paul McCartney
    C. Rod Stewart

86. Who was the first non-English player to participate in the World Cup Finals?
    A. Agustín Delgado
    B. Kenwyne Jones
    C. Chris Nicholl

87. What is the club's official website?
    A. saints.co.uk
    B. saintsfc.co.uk
    C. southamptonfc.com

88. What is the most number of goals scored by the club in the Premier League?
    A. 57
    B. 59
    C. 61

89. Who was the first full time manager of Southampton?
    A. Ted Bates
    B. Arthur Dominy
    C. George Swift

90. Who was the first player to score 150 goals for the club?
    A. Arthur Dominy
    B. Bill Rawlings
    C. Matthew Le Tissier

Here are the answers to the last block of questions.

A81. Albert Brown scored 7 goals in a match against Northampton Town on 28th December 1901, which is the highest number of goals in a single match for the club.

A82. Matt Le Tissier won the Player of the Year Award three times.

A83. On 23 April 2019, Shane Long scored the fastest goal in Premier League history against Watford, clocking in at 7.69 seconds after kick off. Shane Long joined the club from Hull City in August 2014.

A84. Under Armour have manufactured the club's kits since 2016.

A85. Bon Jovi has played two gigs at the stadium; in 2006 and in 2008.

A86. Chris Nicholl was the first non-English Southampton player to participate in the World Cup Finals. He participated in the 1982 World Cup in Spain for Northern Ireland.

A87. Southampton's official website address is saintsfc.co.uk

A88. Southampton scored 61 goals in the 1995/96 season, a record in the Premier League era for the club

A89. George Swift was the first full time manager of Southampton, taking charge in August 1911.

A90. Centre forward Bill Rawlings was the first player to score 150 goals for the club. He played for the club from 1918 to 1928 and finished his career with 175 goals for the club; in 327 appearances.

Here is the final set of questions. Enjoy!

91. Who is the current owner of Southampton?
    A. Gao Jisheng
    B. Katharina Liebherr
    C. Les Reed

92. How many appearances did Mick Channon make for the club?
    A. 607
    B. 623
    C. 639

93. When did the club move to St Mary's Stadium from the Dell?
    A. 2000
    B. 2001
    C. 2002

94. What is the highest ever position attained by Southampton in the First Division?
    A. Second
    B. Third
    C. Fourth

95. Which season is known as the 'Even Season'?
    A. 1920/21
    B. 1922/23
    C. 1924/25

96. Which club was Gareth Bale sold to in 2007?
   A. Chelsea
   B. Real Madrid
   C. Tottenham Hotspur

97. Which year did Southampton reach the First Division for the first time?
   A. 1964
   B. 1966
   C. 1968

98. What shirt number does Ryan Bertrand wear?
   A. 3
   B. 21
   C. 23

99. In which year did a bomb land on the Dell pitch leaving an 18-foot crater?
   A. 1939
   B. 1940
   C. 1942

100. What is the club's best ever finish in the Premier League?
   A. 5th
   B. 6th
   C. 7th

101. Which Southampton legend has a
statue outside the ground?
   A. Ted Bates
   B. Lawrie McMenemy
   C. Matt Le Tissier

Here are the answers to the final set of questions.

A91. A Chinese investor group led by Gao Jisheng purchased an 80% share of the club in August 2017. There are various rumours circulating that they are looking to sell the club.

A92. Mick Channon made 607 appearances for the club.

A93. The club moved to St Mary's Stadium in time for the beginning of the 2001/02 season. The club played their first league game there on 25th August 2001, against Chelsea.

A94. The highest ever position attained by Southampton in the old First Division is second in the 1983/84 season.

A95. The 1922/23 season was known as the "Even Season" as the club recorded 14 wins, 14 draws and 14 defeats. Goals for and against were also equal.

A96. Gareth Bale was sold to Tottenham Hotspur in May 2007.

A97. Southampton reached the First Division for the first time in 1966.

A98. Bertrand wears shirt number 3.

A99. A bomb landed on pitch at the Dell during the Second World War in 1940 leaving an 18 feet wide crater. The bomb damaged an underground culvert and flooded the pitch.

A100. The best position Southampton has finished in the Premier League is sixth. The club reached this position at the end of the 2015/16 season.

A101. There is a wonderful statue of Ted Bates outside the stadium, behind the Itchen Stand. It was unveiled in March 2008. It is the second statue of Bates to be unveiled; as the first statue was simply not up to scratch.

That's it. That's a great question to finish with. I hope you enjoyed this book, and I hope you got most of the answers right.

I also hope you learnt some new facts about the club, and if you spotted anything wrong, or have a general comment, please visit the glowwormpress.com website.

Thanks for reading, and if you did enjoy the book, would you please leave a positive review on Amazon.

Printed in Great Britain
by Amazon